# THE
FACTS ABOUT
CHRISTIANITY

Alison Cooper

HODDER
Wayland

an imprint of Hodder Children's Books

This book is based on the original title *Christianity* by
Carol Watson, in the *What do we know about . . .?*
series, published in 1996 by Macdonald Young Books

This differentiated text version by Alison Cooper, published
in 2004 by Hodder Wayland, an imprint of Hodder
Children's Books
© Hodder Wayland 2004

Original designer and illustrator: Celia Hart
Layout for this edition: Jane Hawkins
Consultant: Jane Clements

Hodder Children's Books
A division of Hodder Headline Limited,
338 Euston Road London NW1 3BH

Photograph acknowledgements: Front cover, Corbis; Ace
Photo Agency, p16; Andes Press Agency, pp13(b), 18, 23(b),
28, 32, 33(t), 37(t), 39(b), 40(1); Bridgeman Art Library,
endpapers, *The Annunciation* and *The Nativity* 1491, after
designs by Domenico Ghirlandaio (1449-94), Santa Maria
delle Carceri, Prato; p12 *The Annunciation* c.1438-45 (fresco)
by Angelico, Fra (Guido di Pietro) (c.1387-1455), Museo di San
Marco Dell' Angelico, Florence; p14 *The Stoning of St Stephen*
c.1605-7 by Domenichino II (Domenico Zamperi) (1581-1641),
Musee Conde, Chantilly, France Giraudon/Bridgeman Art Library;
p17(b) *Martin Luther* by Cranach, Lucas, the elder (1472-1553) City
of Bristol Museum and Art Gallery; p21(t) *Crucifixion* by
Velasquez, Diego Rodriguez de Silva (1599-1660), Prado,
Madrid; p21(b) *The Incredulity of St Thomas* by Strozzi,
Bernado (1581-1644), Museo de Arte, Ponce, Puerto Rico;
p22 *The Ascension* Psalter of Ingeburg, (c.1210), Musee
Conde, Chantilly, France; Britstock IFA, p19(b); Camera Press,
p9; J Allan Cash Photolibrary, p36(b); Cephas Picture Library,
p31(t); Circa Picture Library, pp20(t), 24, 25(r), 27(b), 39(t), 38;
James Davis Travel Photography, p36(t); ET Archive, pp13(t),
15(t), 20(b); Eye Ubiquitous, pp17(t), 35(b); Chris Fairclough
Colour Library, pp8(t), 23(t), 26, 27(t), 29(b), 42; Format
Photographers, p37(b), Harper Collins, p25(1); The Hutchison
Library, pp15(b) (Lesley McIntyre) 29(t), 30, 31(b); Performing Arts
Library, p40(r); Redferns, p41;
Rex Features, pp8(b), 34, 35(t); Tony Stone, p33(b); Trip, p19(t)
(I Burgandinov).

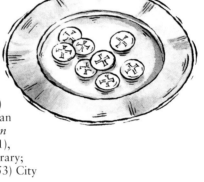

Printed by WKT Company Ltd

A catalogue record of this book is available from the British Library

ISBN 0 750 24592 1

Endpapers: These stained glass windows show two scenes from the New
Testament, *The Annunciation* is on the left and *The Nativity*
is on the right. They were made in CE1491 and are in a church in Italy.

CONTENTS

WHAT IS A CHRISTIAN?

A Christian is someone who believes in Jesus Christ. Jesus was born around 2,000 years ago in Palestine. When he grew up he began to teach people how God wants everyone to live. But when he was 33 years old he was put to death by the Romans. Christians believe that Jesus came to life again after three days. By overcoming death he showed that there is everlasting life with God.

◄ The spread of Christianity

In the 2000 years since Jesus lived, Christianity has spread across the world. There are now more than 1500 million Christians worldwide. The photograph on the left shows African Christians singing and worshipping God together.

Evangelists ►

An evangelist is someone who tells people about Jesus and his teaching, in order to encourage them to become Christians. The photograph on the right shows Billy Graham, a very famous American evangelist. He is preaching to a crowd of thousands of people. Evangelists also use television, books and radio to spread the message of Christianity.

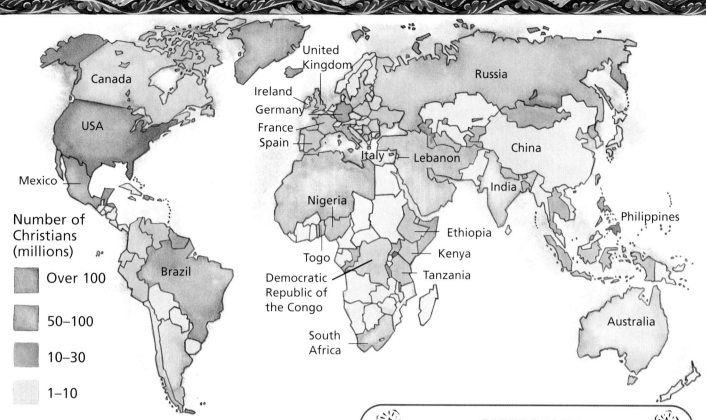

Canada
United
Kingdom
Ireland
Germany
France
Spain
Russia
USA
Italy
Lebanon
China
Mexico
India
Nigeria
Philippines
Number of
Christians
(millions)
Ethiopia
Togo
Kenya
Over 100
Brazil
Democratic
Republic of
the Congo
Tanzania
50–100
Australia
10–30
South
Africa
1–10

The Christian world ▲

This map is a guide to the countries where
Christians live. In some countries nearly
everyone is a Christian. In Mexico for
example there are 93 million Christians,
which is 95 per cent of the population.

DIFFERENT BRANCHES

All Christians are followers of Jesus.
However, there are several groupings within
Christianity – the three main branches are
Orthodox, Roman Catholic and Protestant.
Each branch has slightly different beliefs
and ways of worshipping from the others.

Christian work ▶

Christians believe that the
most important things are to
love God and to carry out
his work in the world by
helping other people.
Monks, nuns, priests and
ministers devote their lives to
serving other people and
spreading the teachings of
Jesus. This nun is visiting a
patient in hospital.

TIMELINE

EVENTS IN CHRISTIANITY

BCE = Before the Common Era = BC (Before Christ)

CE = Common Era = AD
AD = Anno Domini
(the Year of our Lord) =
the years after the birth of Christ

61 BCE	4 BCE	C. CE26	C. CE29	C. CE29 (THREE DAYS LATER)	C. CE29 (FORTY DAYS LATER)	C. CE29 (TEN DAYS LATER)
The Romans occupied Judea (part of Palestine).	Jesus Christ, the Son of God, was born in Bethlehem in Judea.	Jesus began his work of teaching people about God. He chose twelve followers (disciples) to help him.	Jesus was put to death on a cross (crucifixion).	Jesus rose from the dead – this is called the 'Resurrection'.	Jesus went to heaven to be with God. This is called the 'Ascension'.	The disciples received the Holy Spirit. This is the festival of Pentecost.

Roman soldier ▶

Star of Bethlehem ▲

CE1535	CE1534	CE1517	CE1300	CE1209	CE1096	CE1054
Use of an English translation of the bible was allowed in England for the first time.	Henry VIII made himself head of the Church in England.	Martin Luther began the Reformation. Protestant Christianity began.	Christianity had reached Iceland, China and Russia.	St Francis of Assisi founded his order of Franciscan monks.	The Crusades began – Muslims and Christians fought for control of Jerusalem.	The Church split into Orthodox and Roman Catholic branches.

CE1540						
Ignatius Loyola founded the Society of Jesus – the Jesuits.						

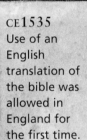

◀ Henry VIII

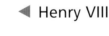

◀ Martin Luther

CE1549	CE1611	CE1620	CE1703	CE1792	CE1858	CE1910
The first English Book of Common Prayer was used.	The Authorised Version of the Bible was published.	English Puritans sailed to America, so that they could be free to worship God as they wished.	John Wesley, founder of Methodism, was born.	The first missionary society in England was founded.	Bernadette began to see visions of the Virgin Mary at Lourdes, France.	The first World Missionary Conference was held.

When historians first worked out the date of Jesus' birth, they got the date wrong by four years. The correct date for the birth of Jesus is therefore c.4BCE, not CE1.

The Messiah

Prophets in ancient Israel promised the Jewish people that God would send a special leader to rescue them from their enemies. Jews believe that this leader or Messiah has not yet come. Christians believe that Jesus was the Messiah and was sent to fulfil God's promise.

c. CE33 Saul was converted to Christianity and his name became Paul.	CE47–60 Paul travelled as a missionary. Followers of Jesus became known as Christians.	CE60–65 Many Christians were put to death by the Roman Emperor Nero.	CE65–100 The Gospels of the New Testament were written.	CE70 Jerusalem was taken over by the Romans.
				CE100 At least 25,000 Christians had been killed for their beliefs by this time.

Paul's ship ▶

CE800 Charlemagne became the first Holy Roman Emperor.	CE313 Emperor Constantine allowed Christians in the Roman Empire to worship freely.	C. CE300 A new group of Christian missionaries arrived in Britain.	C. CE200 Christianity came to Britain.	CE180 Christianity had spread to Persia, North Africa and India.

◀ A statue of Charlemagne

◀ Woman priest

CE1948 The World Council of Churches was founded.	CE1962–5 The Vatican Council began to reform the Roman Catholic Church.	CE1968 The Ecumenical Movement was set up to bring more unity to the Christian Church.	CE1986 The Pope, Archbishop of Canterbury and other faith leaders met to pray for peace.	CE1993 The first women were ordained as priests in the Church of England.

The cross ▲

Jesus was killed by being nailed to a wooden cross. This is called crucifixion. Christians believe that Jesus died so that all people could be forgiven and have a new relationship with God. The cross is a very important symbol for Christians because it is a reminder of the sacrifice Jesus made.

WHAT DO CHRISTIANS BELIEVE?

Christians believe that Jesus was the Son of God. He came into the world to save people from their sins. If people are sorry for things they have done

wrong, God offers them a new life in this world and in heaven after they have died. Christians also believe in the Holy Trinity, which means the three ways in which God is at work in the world – as the Father, the Son and the Holy Spirit.

The birth of Jesus ▲

Jesus was born around 4 BCE. His parents were a Jewish couple, Mary and Joseph. Before Mary married Joseph, an angel appeared and told her she was going to have a baby who would be the Son of God. This event, shown in the painting, is called *The Annunciation*, The angel told Mary to name the child Jesus. Christians call Jesus 'Christ' – this comes from the Greek word *Khristos* and it means the same as the word 'Messiah' in Hebrew, the language of the Jews.

Jesus the teacher and healer ▶

When he was about 30 years old, Jesus began to teach people about God. He chose twelve followers, who were known as his 'disciples'. In the picture on the right you can see Jesus and some of his disciples.

Jesus travelled all over Palestine with his disciples. He performed miracles and healed the sick. He told people to trust God, to obey his laws and to look after the needs of others.

Palestine

This was the name the Romans gave to the Jewish land where Jesus lived and worked.

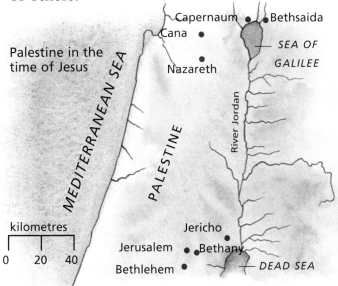

Palestine in the time of Jesus

Capernaum • • Bethsaida
Cana •
Nazareth •
SEA OF GALILEE
MEDITERRANEAN SEA
PALESTINE
River Jordan
Jericho •
Jerusalem • • Bethany
Bethlehem •
DEAD SEA

kilometres
0   20   40

THE GREAT COMMANDMENTS

Jesus gave his followers two commandments or laws to guide them. One was, 'Love the Lord your God with all your heart, and with all your soul, and with all your strength and with all your mind.' The second was 'Love others as yourselves.'

Helping others ▶

Christians believe their skills and talents are a gift from God. These should be used to help other people and spread Jesus' teaching.

Many Christians work with those who need help because of sickness, war or natural disasters. This photograph shows an aid worker with people in Somalia during a famine.

HOW DID CHRISTIANITY BEGIN?

After Jesus died and rose to life again, he appeared to his disciples. He told them to spread his teaching to people everywhere. He promised that God would send his Holy Spirit to give them the strength they needed to carry on his work. The disciples did as Jesus had told them and thousands of people became followers of Jesus. They became known as 'Christians'.

The death of Stephen ▶
Stephen was one of the first Christians. He was a great preacher and healer, and many people came to listen to him. The Jewish leaders saw Jesus and his followers as a threat to them because Jesus' teaching about God was different from their own. Some were afraid that they would lose their power if everyone began to follow Jesus. They arrested Stephen and accused him of speaking against God. The painting shows him being stoned to death. As he died, he cried out, 'Lord, forgive them for what they are doing.'

 MARTYRS
A martyr is a person who is killed because of his beliefs. Stephen was the first Christian martyr but many more of the early Christians were put to death for following Jesus.

◀ Saul becomes a Christian

Saul was determined to stop the spread of Christianity. He killed and persecuted all the Christians he could find. One day he set out along the road to Damascus. The painting on the left shows Jesus appearing to him in a vision. Jesus said, 'Saul, Saul, why are you persecuting me?' Saul was blinded by the vision but a Christian prayed for him and his sight was restored. After this experience, Saul became a Christian too. His name was changed to Paul and he became one of Christianity's greatest leaders.

I	Jesus
X	Christ
Θ	God's
Y	Son
Σ	Saviour

Secret code ▶

It was dangerous for the early Christians to meet, so they used a secret code. They drew half a fish and if someone completed the fish, they knew he or she was a believer too. The letters of the Greek word for fish stood for the words 'Jesus Christ God's Son Saviour'.

Missionaries ▶

Paul became the first Christian missionary. He spread Christianity to people in the lands around the Mediterranean Sea who had never heard of Jesus Christ. Since then, missionaries have taken the Christian faith all over the world. This priest and nun are leading a service in Africa.

WHY ARE THERE DIFFERENT BRANCHES OF CHRISTIANITY?

There are different branches of Christianity because Christians worship in different ways. One reason for this is because of an argument between two powerful Christian leaders. The Patriarch (bishop) of Rome and the

Patriarch of Constantinople (now Istanbul) disagreed about how people should worship and about some beliefs. In 1054 the Patriarch of Rome separated his part of the Church from the rest.

Branches of Christianity ▶

After the *Great Divide* in the Church in 1054, the branch of Christianity led by the Patriarch of Rome became the Catholic Church. The part led by the Patriarch of Constantinople became the Orthodox Church. In the sixteenth century, people set up a new branch called Protestantism.

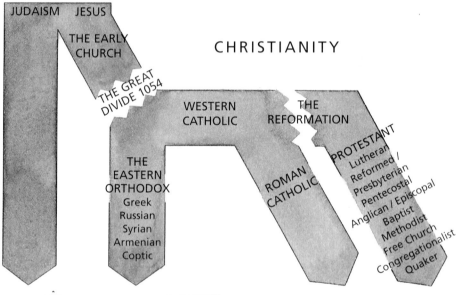

JUDAISM   JESUS

THE EARLY CHURCH

CHRISTIANITY

THE GREAT DIVIDE 1054

WESTERN CATHOLIC

THE REFORMATION

THE EASTERN ORTHODOX
Greek
Russian
Syrian
Armenian
Coptic

ROMAN CATHOLIC

PROTESTANT
Lutheran
Reformed /
Presbyterian
Pentecostal
Anglican / Episcopal
Baptist
Methodist
Free Church
Congregationalist
Quaker

◀ **The Pope**

Today the leader of the Catholic Church is called the Pope instead of the Patriarch. He still has his headquarters in Rome, in the Vatican City. This photograph shows a crowd listening to the Pope, who is speaking from a balcony in the centre of the picture.

Orthodox and Catholic

The word 'catholic' means 'universal'. The word 'orthodox' means 'right belief'. The two branches of Christianity gave themselves these names because each thought that it was the true Church. Catholic services were in Latin, the language of the western Roman empire. Orthodox services were in Greek, the language used in the eastern empire. Leaders of the Orthodox Church are still called patriarchs. This is the Patriarch of Moscow, the head of the Orthodox Church in Russia.

> ### THE VIRGIN MARY
> The Virgin Mary is especially important to Roman Catholics and Orthodox Christians. They pray to her for help because she is the mother of Jesus.

◀ Protestants

The painting on the left shows Martin Luther. He was a German monk who lived in the early 1500s. He thought that the Roman Catholic Church had moved too far away from the teachings of Jesus.

Luther and others protested and called for reform, or changes. They set up their own form of Christianity. They were known as 'Protestants' and their split from the Catholic Church is called the 'Reformation'. Protestant services were held in a language ordinary people could understand, instead of in Latin. Today there are many groups of Protestants, including Anglicans, Methodists and Baptists.

WHAT IS CHRISTMAS?

Christmas is the first festival of the Christian year. It celebrates the birth of Jesus, when Christians believe God came into the world as a person. This is called the 'Incarnation'. Roman Catholics and Protestants celebrate Christmas on 25 December. Eastern Orthodox Christians celebrate the birth of Jesus on 7 January. No-one knows the real date of Jesus' birth.

Christian festivals

Christian festivals are linked to events in the life of Jesus. This chart shows at what time of year they take place.

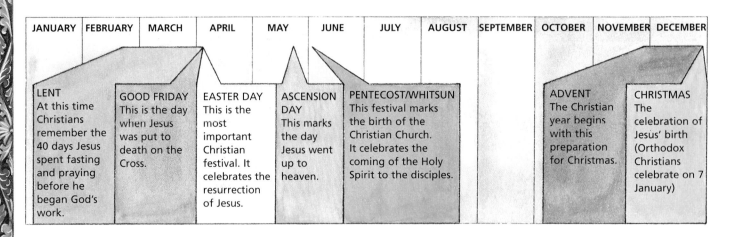

JANUARY	FEBRUARY	MARCH	APRIL	MAY	JUNE	JULY	AUGUST	SEPTEMBER	OCTOBER	NOVEMBER	DECEMBER

LENT
At this time Christians remember the 40 days Jesus spent fasting and praying before he began God's work.

GOOD FRIDAY
This is the day when Jesus was put to death on the Cross.

EASTER DAY
This is the most important Christian festival. It celebrates the resurrection of Jesus.

ASCENSION DAY
This marks the day Jesus went up to heaven.

PENTECOST/WHITSUN
This festival marks the birth of the Christian Church. It celebrates the coming of the Holy Spirit to the disciples.

ADVENT
The Christian year begins with this preparation for Christmas.

CHRISTMAS
The celebration of Jesus' birth (Orthodox Christians celebrate on 7 January)

◀ Advent

Advent begins four Sundays before Christmas. It is the time when Christians look forward to God coming into the world as a person – the word 'Advent' means 'coming'. These children are lighting an Advent candle. One more candle is lit each Sunday until all four burn together. The central candle is lit on Christmas Day.

The birth of Jesus ▶

The story of Jesus' birth is told in the Bible, the Christian holy book. Just before Jesus was born his parents, Mary and Joseph, had to make a long journey to the town of Nazareth. When they arrived all the inns were full, so they sheltered in a stable. Jesus was born there and Mary laid him to sleep in the animals' manger.

Angels appeared to some shepherds nearby and told them the 'Saviour' or 'Messiah' had been born. They came and worshipped the baby. Meanwhile, three wise men, who were probably astronomers, had seen a new star in the sky. They followed the star for many days and it led them to Jesus. They brought him gifts of gold, frankincense and myrrh.

Christmas crib

Christmas worship ▲

These children in Kazakhstan are leaving church on Christmas morning. On Christmas Eve or Christmas Day Christians give thanks to God for sending his Son into the world.

◀ Christmas presents

The people in this photograph are happily unwrapping their Christmas presents. Christians give presents at Christmas to remember that Jesus was God's gift to the world.

WHAT IS EASTER?

Easter Day is the most important Christian festival. It is a celebration of the day Jesus rose from the dead. The 40 days leading up to Easter are called Lent. This is a time when Christians think about things they have done wrong and ask God to forgive them. The week before Easter is called Holy Week. It begins with Palm Sunday.

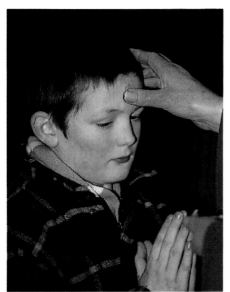

◄ Lent

During Lent Christians remember the 40 days Jesus spent praying and fasting before he began God's work. On Ash Wednesday, the first day of Lent, some people go to church. The priest uses ash to make the sign of the cross on their foreheads. This is to show that God forgives people who are sorry for their sins.

Palm Sunday ►

This marks the day when Jesus rode into Jerusalem on a donkey. Crowds of people waving palm branches welcomed him. Crosses made of palm leaves are given out in churches on this day.

A palm cross

The Last Supper ►

The night before he was crucified, Jesus and his disciples shared a last meal together. This painting shows Jesus washing Peter's feet before the meal begins. This job was usually done by a servant. Jesus did it to show his disciples how important it was to look after other people.

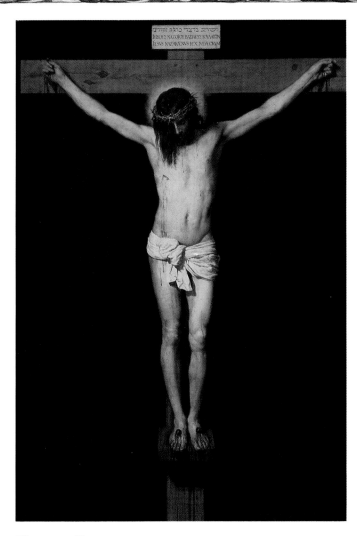

◄ Good Friday

This is the day when Christians remember the death of Jesus on the cross. The name 'Good Friday' probably comes from 'God's Friday', or from a time when 'good' meant 'holy'.

Some Jewish leaders felt threatened by Jesus because his teaching about God was different from theirs. They plotted against him and then handed him over to the Romans who ruled Palestine at that time. The Romans put him to death by nailing him to a cross. This was known as crucifixion.

The greatest sacrifice anyone can make is to die for someone else. Christians believe that Jesus died so that everyone could be forgiven for their sins and have a new relationship with God.

Easter Day ▶

The sadness of Good Friday is followed by the joy of Easter Day. When Jesus' followers came to his tomb on Sunday morning they found it was empty. Jesus had risen from the dead.

This painting shows Jesus appearing to his disciples after his resurrection. He is showing Thomas the wounds he suffered on the cross, to prove that he has really come back to life.

Christians believe that Jesus' resurrection means that when people die, it is not the end. There is everlasting life with God for those who believe in him.

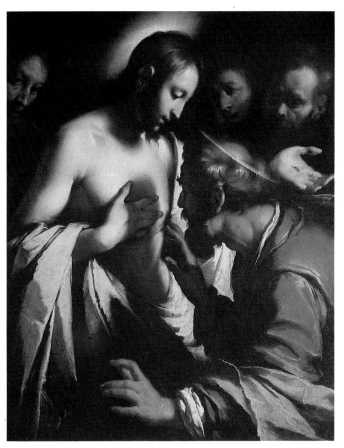

WHAT ARE THE OTHER CHRISTIAN FESTIVALS?

The other two main festivals are Ascension and Pentecost. Some Christians also celebrate several less important festivals. These include saints' days and feast days, such as All Saints' Day and harvest festival. These festivals are celebrated in different ways around the world.

The Ascension ▲

After he rose from the dead, Jesus appeared to his disciples many times. He explained to them that he wanted them to carry on his teaching after he had gone to heaven. One day, he said to them, 'Don't ever forget that, although you can't see me, I am always with you.' Then he was taken up to heaven. This painting shows the disciples looking up as Jesus ascends to heaven. Jesus' ascension is celebrated 40 days after Easter.

Pentecost

Pentecost, which is sometimes called 'Whitsun', is celebrated ten days after Ascension Day. It marks the day when God sent his Holy Spirit to the disciples. They were filled with confidence and joy, and they also found that they could speak in foreign languages. This meant they could spread the message of Jesus to people in other countries.

◀ Gifts of the Spirit ▲

Pentecostals (above) and Charismatics (left) concentrate on experiencing the Holy Spirit in their worship. The Charismatics raise their hands in worship and praise. Some pray for people to be healed, others believe they have the gift of prophecy (seeing events before they happen).

 SAINTS AND SAINTS' DAYS

Some very holy people are known as saints. People who have performed miracles can become saints. People who have died for their faith are sometimes made saints, too. Many saints have a special day of the year when people remember them. Often, this is the day when the saint died.

The picture shows Saint Francis of Assisi, who lived from 1181 to 1226. He set up an order of monks who devoted their lives to helping the poor and sick. Saint Francis is also remembered for his kindness to animals.

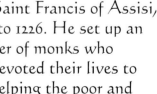

WHAT IS THE CHRISTIANS' HOLY BOOK?

The Christian holy book is called the Bible. Although it looks like one book, it is really a collection of 66 books, written at different times. The books are grouped into two main sections, the Old Testament and the New Testament. Christians believe that the Bible is God's guide to how people should live.

◄ The Old Testament

The word 'testament' means agreement or promise. In the Old Testament (the Jewish Bible) God promised Abraham that he would always look after the Jewish people, as long as they loved him and obeyed his laws.

The photograph shows a cave near the Dead Sea in Israel. Here, in 1947, a shepherd boy found some scrolls in clay pots. They were ancient copies of part of the Old Testament.

Scrolls ►

The Old Testament was written down thousands of years ago, when very few people could read or write. Educated people called scribes used reed pens to write on sheets of papyrus, a kind of paper. The sheets were stuck together to make long scrolls.

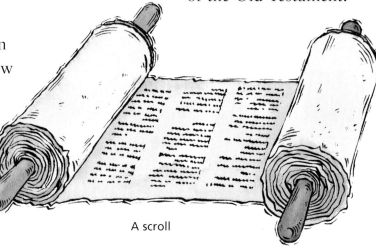

A scroll

The New Testament ▶

The New Testament is about the new promise God made by sending his son Jesus into the world. It tells the story of Jesus' birth, his teaching, and his death and resurrection. It also describes how the Christian faith began and spread, and how Christians believe Jesus will return to the world.

The New Testament was written in Greek by followers of Jesus and early Christians on sheets of parchment bound together at the edges. This was called a 'codex'.

A codex

LUKE

◀ Translating the Bible

The name 'Bible' comes from the Greek word for 'books' – *biblia*. Before printing was invented in the fifteenth century, monks wrote out copies of the Bible in Latin by hand. The photograph on the left shows a page from a Bible written in English. The first authorized English translation of the Bible was produced in 1611. Today the Bible has been translated into nearly 2,000 languages.

Reading the Bible ▶

The minister in the photograph on the right is reading from the Bible during a church service. The holy book rests on a wooden stand called a lectern. All Christians read the Bible. Worship is based on teachings and readings from the Old and New Testaments.

HOW DO CHRISTIANS WORSHIP?

Christians like to meet together to worship. Any group of Christians that meets regularly is called a 'church'. This word is also used for the building where Christians worship.

The main day for worship is Sunday, because this is the day when Jesus rose from the dead. Church services are led by a priest, vicar, minister or other leader. At a service people pray, listen to readings from the Bible and sing songs of praise to God.

The Lord's supper ▲

The photograph above shows priests giving people bread and wine. They are taking part in an important service, which different groups of Christians call by different names: Mass, Holy Communion, the Eucharist or the Lord's Supper. It is a reminder of the last meal Jesus and his disciples shared. Jesus passed round bread and wine. He said that these were his body and blood, which he was going to sacrifice to pay for the sins of all people.

Altar cross

◄ Songs of praise

The photograph on the left shows a choir singing a psalm from the Bible. A choir is a group of adults and children with beautiful voices, who lead the singing. In an Orthodox service the priest and the choir sing the whole service and the congregation usually stand and listen.

Sermons and talks ►

The sermon, homily or talk is an important part of many Christian services. The photograph on the right shows a vicar preaching from the pulpit. The pulpit is raised up on a platform, so that everyone can hear and see the preacher. The sermon is often based on the section of the Bible that has been read earlier in the service. The preacher explains the message of the Bible so that the congregation can learn how to live their lives in a Christian way.

CONFESSION

Confession is when Christians say sorry to God for the things they have done wrong and ask to be forgiven. Confession is important for all Christians, so that they can have a close relationship to God.

WHERE DO CHRISTIANS WORSHIP?

Many Christians meet in buildings made especially for worship. These range from enormous cathedrals to tiny chapels. Many churches face east because the rising sun is a symbol for the resurrection of Jesus. Usually there is a table called an altar at the eastern end of the church, decorated with a cross and candles.

◀ Cathedrals

A cathedral is a very large church. The photograph on the left shows the Roman Catholic cathedral in London. The cathedral is beautifully decorated with many candles and paintings. A large crucifix – a cross with a picture or carving of Jesus on it – hangs from the ceiling.

A stained glass window from Chartres Cathedral.

Stained glass windows ▶

Often, churches have beautiful windows of coloured, or 'stained', glass. These show scenes from the life of Jesus or pictures of saints. They were first used at a time when few people could read the Bible – priests used the pictures to tell the story of Jesus.

Parish churches ▶

The photograph on the right is of a parish church in England. Many churches have a tower or steeple at the west end that can be seen from far away. Inside, people sit in rows on chairs or wooden benches called pews. These face the altar. In an Orthodox church the altar is behind a screen.

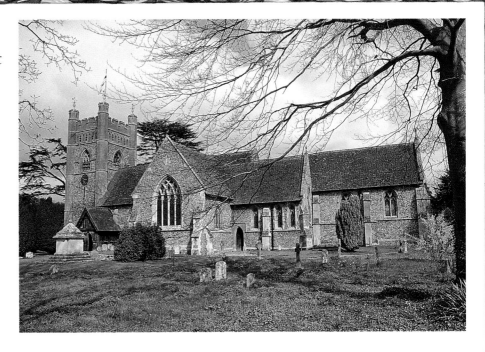

Simple churches ▲

The small African church above was built from materials people could find in the local area. The cross above the door is the only sign that it is a place where Christians worship. Churches do not have to be grand buildings. The faith of the people who meet there is most important.

FREE CHURCHES

Free churches are often called 'Non-conformist' churches. Their members do not 'conform' to, or follow, any set way of worshipping but worship in the way they choose. There are also 'house' churches where Christians meet in each other's homes.

WHY DO CHRISTIANS PRAY?

Prayer is the way Christians talk and listen to God. They pray to thank or praise God. They might pray for God's help for themselves or other people, or for forgiveness for things they have done wrong. They believe that if it is God's will, their prayers will be answered.

Christians stand, kneel, sit or lie face down to pray. They might put their hands together or hold them up towards God. Some make the sign of the cross in front of their bodies.

THE LORD'S PRAYER

Jesus taught this prayer to his disciples. It contains all the different kinds of prayer – praise and asking for help and forgiveness. All Christians use this prayer.

Praying together ▲

These Christian children in India are praying together at the start of their school day. School children all over the world pray and sing to God in assembly. Some also pray before their school meal, to thank God for their food.

The prayer used before a meal is often called 'Grace'.

Our father in heaven,
hallowed be your name,
your kingdom come,
Your will be done,
on earth as in heaven.
Give us today our daily bread.
Forgive us our sins, as we forgive
those who sin against us.
Lead us not into temptation,
but deliver us from evil.
For the kingdom, the power and
the glory are yours,
now and for ever. Amen.

Praying in church ▶

This photograph shows a small boy leading the prayers in church. He is standing at the centre of the photograph with the minister beside him. Christians support and encourage each other by praying together. They pray for one another, for people in their local community and for people around the world suffering from war, famine or other disasters.

◀ Praying alone

Many Christians pray on their own every day. They find it gives them strength to cope with life. Some people light a candle and place it near a holy statue or picture. The woman in the photograph on the left is praying in an Orthodox church in Russia. She is making the sign of the cross, as a reminder of how Jesus died.

Prayer book and rosary ▶

Some Christians use a book of prayers to help them pray. Some use a rosary – a string of beads with a cross on the end. They start at the cross and say a prayer. They say a different prayer as they touch each bead.

Rosary

Prayer book

WHAT ARE THE MAIN CHRISTIAN CELEBRATIONS?

Christians believe that they are members of one big family – the worldwide community of Christians. By marking the important stages in their lives

with their Christian family, they can share their joy in happy times and receive support in times of sadness. The main Christian celebrations are baptism, first communion (celebrated by Roman Catholics), confirmation, marriage and death.

Baptism ▶

The priest on the right is baptising a baby. He sprinkles water over the baby's forehead. Using the baby's first or 'Christian' name, he says 'I baptise you in the name of the Father, and of the Son, and of the Holy Spirit.' Then he makes the sign of the cross on the baby's forehead.

The baptism ceremony is the way that people become accepted into the church. Jesus was baptised in the River Jordan and he told his followers to baptise others. Water is used in the ceremony to show that the person's sins have been 'washed away' and they are starting a new life with Jesus Christ. In some churches people are baptised in a deep pool of water.

Confirmation ▶

At this ceremony young people or adults 'confirm' that they want to become members of the Christian Church. In the photograph on the right the bishop is using holy oil to mark the boy's forehead with the sign of the cross.

FIRST COMMUNION

Roman Catholic children take part in a ceremony called First Communion between the ages of seven and nine. This means they are allowed to receive the bread and wine during Mass, even though they have not yet been confirmed.

◀ Marriage

The photograph on the left shows a wedding. The couple who are getting married make solemn promises to one another and receive a blessing. Christians believe that God wants a husband and wife to be united in love throughout their lives, just as Jesus is united with those who follow him in Christianity.

Death ▶

Christians believe that a Christian who has died has gone to heaven to be with Jesus. They mark the person's death with a funeral service of prayers, Bible readings and hymns. The person's body may be cremated (burned), or buried and marked with a gravestone.

A gravestone

WHO ARE THE LEADERS OF THE CHRISTIAN CHURCH?

The first leaders of the Christian Church were the twelve disciples of Jesus. As the church spread into other lands, each new area of Christians had its own leader, called a patriarch (bishop). Today, a bishop leads a group of churches in an area called a diocese. The diocese is divided into smaller areas called parishes, each led by a priest, vicar or minister.

A bishop of the Eastern Orthodox Church ▼

Mitre

Crozier

Robes

The Pope ▲

The photograph above shows Pope John Paul II. The Pope is the leader of the Roman Catholic Church. Roman Catholics believe that his authority comes directly from Peter, the disciple of Jesus. Jesus said to him, 'You are Peter, the Rock; and on this rock I will build my church.' Many believe that Peter was the first Bishop of Rome.

Patriarchs ▶

There are several branches of the Orthodox Church, including the Greek Orthodox Church and the Russian Orthodox Church. The Orthodox churches do not have one overall leader. Each branch is led by a patriarch and all the patriarchs have equal authority. This is the elaborate clothing worn by Orthodox bishops.

Archbishops

The dioceses of bishops are grouped together into provinces. The bishop of the principal diocese may be called an archbishop. The photograph on the right shows George Carey who was Archbishop of Canterbury from 1991 to 2003. The Archbishop of Canterbury is the senior Archbishop of the Church of England. He is also the leader of all Anglicans worldwide.

Priests and ministers

Men and women who want to become priests or ministers train at a theological college. Here, they study the Bible, discuss religious issues and learn about the role of priests in the community. When they have completed their training they are blessed by the bishop and given the authority to work as priests at a service called 'ordination'. Above are some of the first women to be ordained in the Church of England. Some branches of the Christian Church do not allow women to become priests.

Parish priests may be in charge of one or more churches. They 'minister' to, or serve, the people who attend their church and also people in their local community. They visit the sick and elderly and try to help people as much as they can.

OTHER LEADERS

There are certain ceremonies, such as baptism and the giving of holy communion, that can only be carried out by ordained priests. But other Christians can lead worship and preach to the congregation.

WHICH ARE THE CHRISTIAN HOLY PLACES?

A holy place is one that is connected with events in the life of Jesus or a Christian saint. The area where Jesus lived and worked is known as the

'Holy Land'. Places where saints have had visions, performed miracles or been buried are holy places too. Some Christians make journeys, called 'pilgrimages', to holy places, to give thanks to God, or to ask for forgiveness or to be healed.

◀ Jerusalem

The photograph on the left shows Jerusalem, in Israel. This is a holy city for Christians, Jews and Muslims. Christians believe that Jesus was crucified and rose from the dead in Jerusalem. They also believe it was here that the disciples received the gift of the Holy Spirit. So it is the place where the Christian Church began. Believers have made pilgrimages to Jerusalem since the earliest days of Christianity.

St Peter's in Rome ▶

The photograph on the right shows St Peter's Church in Rome. It is a beautiful building full of sculptures and paintings. Christians believe that Jesus' disciple Peter was the first Bishop of Rome. Like Jesus, he was crucified by the Romans. According to tradition, he is buried in the place where his church now stands.

The shrine at Walsingham

Lourdes ▲

The shrine of the Virgin Mary at Lourdes in France. In 1858 a girl called Bernadette said she had seen visions of the Virgin Mary at this spot. Later, a spring of water appeared, which some people believe has healing powers. These people are pilgrims hoping to be healed.

MIRACLES AND HEALING

Miracles have been performed in the name of Jesus since Christianity first began. People have been healed of illnesses and disabilities. Sometimes these miracles have taken place at holy places, which is one reason why people visit them.

Walsingham ▲

The shrine of the Virgin Mary at Walsingham in Norfolk, UK, was founded 1,000 years ago. The water from the well here is believed to have the same healing power as the water at Lourdes. Although the shrine was destroyed in the 1500s, it was rebuilt in the twentieth century.

Convents and monasteries ▶

Nuns, like the ones in this photograph, and monks are people who devote their lives to serving God within a religious community. The convents and monasteries where they live are peaceful places. Some people like to visit them for a short period of quiet thought and prayer. This is called a 'retreat'.

WHAT OBJECTS ARE USED IN CHRISTIAN WORSHIP?

For Christians, the feeling in their heart that they want to worship God is more important than the type of ceremony or the use of special objects. The objects that are used vary from church to church because the different

branches of Christianity have slightly different beliefs and ceremonies. All Christians have ceremonies linked to the sacraments of baptism and holy communion. A sacrament is a visible sign of a spiritual event taking place inside the worshipper.

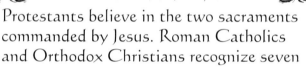

THE SACRAMENTS

Protestants believe in the two sacraments commanded by Jesus. Roman Catholics and Orthodox Christians recognize seven sacraments.

Font and candle ▲

The holy water used in baptism is contained in the font in many churches. The candle is lit during the baptism service to show that the person has passed from darkness into the light of life with Jesus.

The Two Sacraments
(commanded by Jesus)
• Baptism
• The Lord's Supper

The Seven Sacraments
(followed by Roman Catholics and Orthodox Christians)
• Baptism
• Confirmation
• The Lord's Supper
• Penance
• Extreme unction (anointing the sick and dying)
• Holy orders (ordination of bishops, priests and deacons)
• Marriage

Bread and wine ▶

The photographs show a chalice and a paten. These are used to hold the bread and wine during the ceremony of the Lord's Supper (see page 28). Protestants believe the bread and wine are symbols of Christ's body and blood. Roman Catholics and Orthodox Christians believe that the bread and wine actually become the body and blood of Christ through a miraculous process called 'transubstantiation'.

Chalice

Paten

Incense ▶

Some Christians use incense in their ceremonies. Burning incense gives off a sweet-smelling smoke. This symbolizes people's prayers rising to God.

The incense is carried in a thurible

◀ Holy oil

In ancient times prophets anointed with holy oil the people chosen by God to be kings of Israel. Holy oil is still used today. The priest in this photograph is anointing a sick person with oil. This is called the 'sacrament of unction'. Some Christians also use holy oil during baptisms and confirmation ceremonies.

IS MUSIC IMPORTANT TO CHRISTIANS?

Many Christians use music to worship God and celebrate the birth and resurrection of Jesus. Anglicans and Roman Catholics might use a mixture of traditional hymns and psalms and modern music in their services. Pentecostals and Charismatics often have music groups with instruments

such as electric guitars. Orthodox Christians do not use instruments – their services are sung by the priest and choir. Some Christians, such as the Society of Friends, do not use any music at all.

◀ Gregorian chants

In the early Church, Christians probably chanted their songs of praise, without any instruments to accompany them. This style of singing is called 'plainsong', or 'Gregorian chant', after Pope Gregory, who died in CE 604. Gregory was famous for the choirs he set up in Roman churches. The monks in the photograph on the left are chanting plainsong.

Choirs ▶

The photograph on the right shows a cathedral choir. Choirs lead the singing of the congregation and also sing alone. Famous composers such as Mozart, Haydn, Bach, Handel and Britten composed beautiful pieces of music to be performed in churches.

Organ music ▶

Many churches have an organ, which is played before, during and after the service. Organs have been used in churches since the Middle Ages. Only one person is needed to play the keyboard but the grand sound produced by the organ pipes swells to fill even the largest cathedral with music.

A church organ

Gospel music ▲

The singers in the photograph above are Gospel singers. Gospel music is a mixture of traditional hymns and spirituals. The singers sway, dance and clap their hands. Gospel music is especially associated with Pentecostal churches but is used in many other churches as well.

THE SALVATION ARMY

William and Catherine Booth founded the Salvation Army in London in 1878. They wanted a Christian 'army' to fight against sin and poverty. Today the Salvation Army helps the poor and homeless everywhere. In their services they use joyful music, accompanied by instruments and enthusiastic hand-clapping. They often hold services in the open air, to attract crowds to listen to the word of God.

IS STORYTELLING IMPORTANT TO CHRISTIANS?

The Bible is full of stories. They have been told and retold over thousands of years, and written down in ancient scrolls. Many of them are exciting stories of people's lives. Christians believe that the stories in the Bible help them to understand what God is like.

For most Christians the greatest story in the Bible is the story of Jesus himself. There are also many stories that Jesus told to his followers. Some of these are called 'parables'.

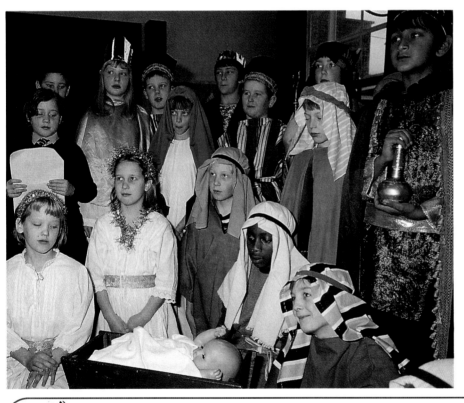

◀ **Nativity plays**
The children in this photograph are performing in a nativity play. This is a play that tells the story of Jesus' birth. The children are dressed up as Mary, Joseph, the shepherds and the wise men who came to visit the baby Jesus. Every year children all over the world act out this story at Christmas time.

PARABLES

A parable is sometimes called 'an earthly story with a heavenly meaning'. It is a story about things that happen in everyday life, but it has a deeper meaning for people who listen carefully. Jesus used this kind of story to help people understand and remember his teaching.

One of the stories that Jesus told is the Parable of the Sower, which is retold on the opposite page. You can find this story in Chapter 8 of St Luke's Gospel, in the New Testament section of the Bible.

The parable of the sower

'Listen to this story,' Jesus said. 'A farmer once went out to sow seed in the fields. Some seed fell on the path and the birds quickly ate it up. Some fell on rocky ground, where there was not much soil. The plants that grew there had only shallow roots, so when the hot sun dried out the ground the plants soon died. Some seed fell among thorns. When the plants grew the thorns choked them, so they could not produce fruit. Then there was the seed that fell on good soil. The plants took root and grew up strong. They produced a good harvest.'

Jesus' followers were puzzled by the story, so Jesus explained what he meant. 'The farmer is the teacher who spreads God's message and the seed is the word of God. Some people are like the seed that fell on the path. As soon as they hear God's word the Devil comes along and they quickly forget all about God.

'Other people are like the seed sown on rocky ground. They hear God's message but their faith is not deep-rooted. They soon give up on God when people hurt them because of their faith. Then there are people like the seed sown among thorns. They let the worries of everyday life crowd out God from their hearts.

'Finally,' said Jesus, 'there are the people like the seed sown in good soil. They take God's message into their hearts and their faith is deep-rooted and strong. They live good lives and show other people that they are obeying God.'

GLOSSARY

Angel A messenger of God.

Anglicans People who follow the beliefs and style of worship of the Church of England.

Ascension When Jesus was taken up to heaven, 40 days after he rose from the dead.

Bishop The overall leader of a group of churches in an area called a diocese.

Church of England The official Church in England. It was created in the 1530s when King Henry VIII refused to recognize the authority of the Pope and it developed into a Protestant church. It is led by the Archbishop of Canterbury.

Congregation People who have gathered together for worship and to listen to a preacher.

Crucifixion Putting someone to death by fastening them to a cross and leaving them to die in the heat of the sun. Jesus was killed in this way.

Gospels The first four books of the New Testament – Matthew, Mark, Luke and John – which tell the story of Jesus' life, teachings and death.

Holy Communion A religious service also known as Mass, the Eucharist and the Lord's Supper. Worshippers are given bread and wine to remind them of the last meal Jesus ate with his disciples. It is also a reminder of the sacrifice Jesus made by dying on the cross.

Methodism A type of Protestant worship set up in the eighteenth century by John Wesley. Methodist churches are Nonconformist churches.

Minister The name usually given to a church leader (priest) in Nonconformist Churches.

Miracle An event that seems impossible, such as making a blind person see, which people believe has been performed by God or a saint.

Missionary Someone who tries to convert people to their own beliefs by teaching about their faith.

Monk A man who chooses to join a religious community instead of having a family life, and promises to spend his life serving God.

Nun A woman who chooses to join a religious community instead of having a family life, and promises to spend her life serving God.

Ordination The religious service at which people are given the authority to work as priests, vicars or ministers.

Palestine The area of the Middle East where Jesus lived. On a modern map the area includes Israel, Jordan and parts of Lebanon and Syria.

Pope The leader of the Roman Catholic Church.

Preach To give a religious talk, to help people to understand the faith and how they should live as followers of the faith.

Prophet Someone who expresses the word of God.

Reformation The events that took place in the early sixteenth century, when Martin Luther and others broke away from the Roman Catholic Church and established Protantism.

Resurrection Rising from the dead. Jesus came to life again on the third day after his death on the cross.

Shrine A place where people come to worship. Often it is the burial place or home of a holy person.

Spirituals Religious songs that began among African slaves in America.

INDEX